■ ShellToolBox 3.0

The Tools You Need For Working At The Linux Shell

Robert Wohlfahrt

From the desk of Robert Wohlfahrt

Dresden, Germany
May 2024

Dear Friend,

I originally wrote this book in 2018, primarily as a reference for Linux command-line tools that can be used to write portable shell scripts for Linux or Unix-like systems.

Over the past few years, more and more questions came up about creating an overview of all the tools necessary for daily work at the Linux command line. This includes not only shell scripting itself but also administrative tasks like system maintenance, user management or permission handling.

Instead of creating a second book, I decided to expand the original edition to cover nearly everything a typical Linux administrator needs on a day-to-day basis

In this book I've organized the tools mainly by usage scenario. And because some tools are really useful in multiple different ways, you'll simply find them within multiple chapters. That's not a bug but a feature ;-)

This book is *not* a compilation of all the available Linux commands (for that, search for executable files on your system). Instead, it focuses on tools that are useful for almost anyone working at the Linux command line on a daily basis (and are available on most systems by default).

If you find a missing tool that is essential for the daily work or administration of a Linux system, or that is particularly useful in typical shell scripts, and this tool is portable across many or most Linux distributions ideally without additional installations, then feel free to reach out to me. (for contact information, see https://robertw.io)

Robert

Table Of Contents

First Steps

If you are for the first time on a Linux system, then here are the essential tools to give you a first impression and to reboot and shutdown the system.

pwd	print the current working directory
pwd --help help pwd	Where are you currently working, in which directory? Use pwd to get this information:

```
max@demo:~$ pwd
/home/max
```

Here you are currently working within the directory "/home/max". Every file or directory you reference from here without giving an absolute path (a path starting with "/") will be referenced relatively from this directory.

Many commands will use this directory as the default directory.

The special directory "." will always point to this directory.

example: copy the file /etc/passwd into the current directory:

```
max@demo:~$ cp /etc/passwd .
max@demo:~$ ls
passwd
```

ls	list the content of a directory
ls --help man ls	ls gives you a list of files within the given directory.

```
ls /tmp
```

If ls is called without a file or directory as a parameter, then the content of the current directory will be listed.

```
ls
```

The most known and used command-line options of ls are probably "-l" and "-a".

While "-l" gives you a detailed listing with meta-information such as owner and timestamps, the "-a" parameter lists also "hidden" files (filenames that starts with a ".")

```
ls -la /tmp
```

sorting: ls can also be used to sort the listing e.g. based on size ("-S") or timestamp ("-t").

```
ls -lt
```

cd	change the current directory
cd --help help cd	With cd you switch the directory where you are currently working in:

```
max@demo:~$ cd /tmp
max@demo:/tmp$
```

Using cd - switches you back to the last directory you where in:

```
max@demo:/tmp$ cd -
/home/max
max@demo:~$ cd -
/tmp
```

if you want to move one directory level "up", use cd ..

```
max@demo:/tmp$ cd ..
max@demo:/$
```

Not only for cd: If you use the special name "~" for referencing a directory, then this *always* points to the home-directory of the current active user:

```
max@demo:/tmp$ cd ~
max@demo:~$
```

and even better, the "~"-sign lets you reference the home-directory of every user, if you prepend the username with it:

```
max@demo:~$ cd ~robert
max@demo:/home/robert$
```

if you call cd without any parameter, you will always jump into the home-directory of the current active user:

```
max@demo:/somewhere/deep/in/the/system$ cd
max@demo:~$
```

whoami	shows the name of the current user

whoami --help
man whoami
	The name says it all: whoami prints out the username of the user that calls this command (aka the current active user in the shell).
	
	```max@demo:~$ whoami```
	```max```

id	shows the identity and the group-memberships of a user

id --help
man id
	id prints out the user-name and id of the currently logged in user and all of its group-memberships
	
	```max@demo:~$ id```
	```uid=1001(max) gid=1001(max) groups=1001(max),27(sudo)```
	
	id can also be used to print this information for a different user
	
	```max@demo:~$ id root```
	```uid=0(root) gid=0(root) groups=0(root)```

groups	shows the group-memberships of a user
groups --help man groups	groups prints out all the groups a user (or the current user) is member of

```
max@demo:~$ groups
max sudo

max@demo:~$ groups root
root
```

w	get the uptime, the load-average and currently logged in users

w --help

man w

The command w gives you a great first view into what's going on on a system.

The output in the following example might be truncated due to space restrictions:

```
max@demo:~$ w
 09:06:07 up 72 days,  1:36,  1 user,  load average:
 USER     TTY      FROM                  LOGIN@   IDLE   JCPU
 max      pts/0    34.90.189.110         08:39    1.00s  0.03s
```

df	show the currently mounted filesystems and their fill-level

df --help

man df

Use df to see all currently mounted filesystems and their fill-level:

```
max@demo:~$ df
Filesystem       1K-blocks    Used Available Use% Mounted o
/dev/xvda1       24638844 2732756  20647848  12% /
udev               494380       4    494376   1% /dev
tmpfs              201528     276    201252   1% /run
```

If you want to see the used and free disk-space in a more "human readable" format instead of "blocks", use the "-h" switch for the "human readable" format:

```
max@demo:~$ df -h
Filesystem       Size  Used Avail Use% Mounted on
/dev/xvda1       24G   2.7G  20G  12% /
udev             483M  4.0K 483M   1% /dev
tmpfs            197M  276K 197M   1% /run
```

reboot	reboots the system
reboot --help man reboot	To reboot the system, simply run `reboot` as the root user: ``` max@demo:~$ sudo reboot ```

halt	shuts down the system
halt --help man halt	to shut down and switch off the system, halt can be used ``` max@demo:~$ sudo halt ```

shutdown	reboots or shuts down the system with an announcemen
shutdown --help man shutdown	With "shutdown" you can reboot or shut down a system with an upfront broadcast announcement to all logged in users. **example:** reboot (with "-r") in 15 minutes: ``` shutdown -r +15 "rebooting in 15 minutes" ``` **example:** shutdown the system (with "-h") at 10:30: ``` shutdown -h 10:30 "the system goes off @10:30" ``` You can cancel a pending shutdown with "-c": ``` shutdown -c ```

File Operations

As a Linux-system often follows the paradigm "everything is a file", the tools for working with files are the most important tools to know. As most of the tools by default do not ask for confirmation, be careful if you work with productive-data and double-check your command-lines before hitting "enter".

touch	generate a new file or update the timestamps of an existing one

touch --help
man touch
	While the main purpose of **touch** is to update the timestamps of a file (aka to "touch" it), you can use it to easily create a new one.
	
	This can be very handy, for instance, if you want to check, if you have permissions to write into a directory - or - if you just need a new file ...
	
	example: update the timestamp of a file or create a new one:
	
	`touch /tmp/newfile.txt`
	
	The new file will have a size of "0" - it won't have any content.
	
	example: update only the modification-time of an existing file and let the other timestamps alone:
	
	`touch -m report.txt`

echo	generate a new file with content or append to an existing one

help echo	In combination with the output-redirection of the shell, the **echo** command can be used to generate a new file with content:
	
	`echo "new file content" > newfile.txt`
	
	or to append additional data to an existing file:
	
	`echo "content to append" >> newfile.txt`

vi	edit the content of a file
vi --help man vi (vimtutor)	The vi is a very powerful text-editor for the command line.

Because of its historical roots, the usage of vi is for most beginners … uhm … horrifying.

But many long-term Linux users (me included) don't want to use a different editor because of its powerful features.

The basics you need to know:

Start to edit a file by simply calling vi with the name of the file you want to edit:

```
vi names.txt
```

After opening, the vi is in "command-mode".

Take the cursor-keys to go to the line you want to change and **hit "i" to enter the "insert-mode".**

Now you can enter any text into the active line.

Leave the "insert-mode" by hitting "<esc>".

Now you can choose and edit another line like described above or you leave the vi in one of the following ways:

- enter ":**wq**" (+ <enter>) to save your changes
- enter ":**q!**" (+ <enter>) to exit without saving your edits
- enter ":**q**" (+ <enter>) to exit if you don't have changed anything

On many Linux distributions the vim is installed ("vi improved") and reachable via the "vi" command.

If so - then chances are high that the command vimtutor is available. This command gives you a really great introduction into the usage of vi(m) via "learning by doing".

Give it a try!

```
vimtutor
```

nano	edit the content of a file
nano --help man nano	nano is a mostly self-explaining editor for textfiles at the command line, that is by default installed on many Linux systems. So if you don't want to mess around with the good old vi, try to use nano:

```
nano names.txt
```

mktemp	generate a new file with a unique, hard to predict filename
mktemp --help man mktemp	Often it can be useful to generate a temporary file with a hard to predict, non existent filename. mktemp prints out the name of the generated file:

```
max@demo:~$ mktemp
/tmp/tmp.XFpjy5GWzz
```

you can give a pattern (template) for how the filename shall be generated:

```
max@demo:~$ mktemp /tmp/mydata_XXXXXX
/tmp/mydata_dLY0zF
```

Typically you will use this command within scripts. Then you have to store the name of the generated file within a variable to use it later on:

```
TEMP=$(mktemp /tmp/mydata_XXXXXX)
echo "brand new content" > $TEMP
```

cat	print out the content of a file
cat --help man cat	if you simply want to print out the content of a file to the console, use cat with the name of the file:

```
cat /etc/passwd
```

You can even print multiple files at the same time, one after the other:

```
cat /etc/passwd /etc/profile
```

This can become very handy for instance, if want to concatenate multiple files into a single one:

```
cat data1 data2 data3 > all_data
```

For doing the opposite - splitting a single file into multiple parts - have a look a `split`.

`cat` can also be used to mark special characters that wouldn't be recognized otherwise:

```
cat -A /etc/profile
```

`cat` will show TAB characters as "^I", line-endings as "$" and other nonprinting characters with "^M-...".

more	a "pager": print out the content of a file page by page
more --help man more	if you are interested in the content of a larger file, you can use `more` instead of `cat`:

```
more /etc/profile
```

use **<enter>** to scroll down one single line or**<space>** to scroll down a whole page.

Hit "q" to quit the `more` command before reaching the end of the file.

`more` can also be used to watch the output of a command:

```
ls -lR /etc | watch
```

less	the better pager: interactively view the content of a file
less --help man less	If you are scrolling through text with the more command, you are not able to scroll backwards. But fortunately, there is a better more installed on most system: the pager less:

```
less /etc/profile
```

Just as with more - you can scroll through the content with <space> and <enter>.

But, why should you? Just use the cursor-keys or page-up page-down to navigate through the shown content - even backwards!

You can even search: try it out by hitting "/". (hint: to jump through all findings, try out the keys "n" and "N" after your first search)

And of course you can use less for watching the output of a command line too:

```
ls -lR /etc | less
```

Leave the less command by simply hitting "q".

tail	print out the last lines of a file
tail --help man tail	If you want to have a look into a larger file, then sometimes only the last few lines of that file are of interest.

By default, tail shows you the last 10 lines of a file:

```
tail /var/log/syslog
```

If you want to, you can set the number of lines you want to see with the "-n" switch:

```
max@demo:~$ tail -n 1 /etc/passwd
max:x:1000:1000:Max:/home/max:/bin/bash
```

For logfiles the "follow-mode" can be really useful: It keeps the file open and shows newly arriving lines in real-time:

```
tail -f /var/log/syslog
```

you can end this "follow-mode" by hitting**<ctrl>-c**

head	print out the first lines of a file
head --help man head	sometimes not the last, but the first lines of a file are of interest:

```
head /etc/profile
```

By default, head will print out the first 10 lines of the file. If you need a different number, use the "-n" switch with **head**.

example: show only the first three lines of "/etc/profile":

```
max@demo:~$ head -n 3 /etc/profile
# /etc/profile

# System wide environment and startup programs, for login
```

wc	count the lines, words and characters within a file
wc --help man wc	The name "wc" stands for "word count". This tool lets you count the words, lines and characters (or bytes if you need) of a file or datastream.

example: count only the lines (switch "-l") of "/etc/passwd":

```
max@demo:~$ wc -l /etc/passwd
34
```

example: How many words are in "/etc/profile"?

```
max@demo:~$ wc -w /etc/profile
277
```

cut	cut lines from a file into parts at a given delimiter
cut --help man cut	**cut** lets you extract one or multiple fields from a file, if the fields in the lines are separatable by a single character or tab.

With "-d" you set the delimiter (if not a TAB) and with "-f" the fields you want to extract.

example: extract only the username (field 1) and the login-shell (field 7) from "/etc/passwd":

```
cut -d : -f 1,7 /etc/passwd
```

cp	copy a file
cp --help man cp	Do you need a copy from a file? Use cp.

example: create a copy with a different name:

```
cp report.txt report_2020.txt
```

example: create a copy with the same name in a different directory:

```
cp report.txt /tmp/
```

If you want to use cp as a sort of backup, then you'll typically need the options "-r" and "-p".

While "-r" is for copying also directories recursively, "-p" is used to preserve all the meta-information of a file if possible (owner, timestamps, ...)

```
cp -pr /home/max /tmp
```

mv	move or rename a file
mv --help man mv	If you want to rename a file or move it to a different location, use mv

```
mv report.txt report_old.txt

mv report.txt archive/
```

ln	create a link

ln --help
man ln
	ln lets you create symbolic-links or hard-links.
	
	Creating a hard-link only works for files (not directories) and within the same filesystem:
	
	`ln report.txt a_second_name.txt`
	
	If you want to create links for directories or between different filesystems, you have to create symbolic-links (often also called "soft-links").
	
	create a symbolic-link with the "-s" switch:
	
	`ln -s /etc/passwd ~/my_name_for_passwd`

rsync	synchronize files from a source to a destination

rsync --help
man rsync
	Even though rsync was made for transferring files over the network, you can also use this tool for local-only data.
	
	rsync can be used to copy only modification from a source to a target - the target will be "synchronized" to the source.
	
	To really transfer every kind of files, to transfer recursively entire directories and to preserve meta-information where possible, use the "archive-mode" with "-a".
	
	`rsync -a working_data/ /srv/backup_01`
	
	rsync does only delete files within the target, if you tell it to do so with the "--delete" switch:
	
	`rsync -a --delete working_data/ /srv/backup_01`

mkdir	create an empty directory
mkdir --help man mkdir	Need a new directory? Create it with mkdir: `mkdir /tmp/pictures`

The directory, where the new directory shall be created in, has to exist beforehand.

If it doesn't, you can create the whole path if needed, by using the "-p" switch:

```
mkdir -p ~/pictures/2020/summer
```

ls	list the content of a directory

ls --help
man ls
	ls gives you a list of files within the given directory.
	
	`ls /tmp`
	
	If ls is called without a file or directory as a parameter, then the content of the current directory will be listed.
	
	`ls`
	
	The most known and used command-line options of ls are probably "-l" and "-a".
	While "-l" gives you a detailed listing with meta-information such as owner and timestamps, the "-a" parameter lists also "hidden" files (filenames that starts with a ".")
	
	`ls -la /tmp`
	
	sorting: ls can also be used to sort the listing e.g. based on size ("-S") or timestamp ("-t").
	
	`ls -lt`

file	get the type of a file
file --help man file	If you want to know the type of a file without analyzing it "by hand", use file:

```
max@demo:~$ file report_exported
report_exported: PDF document, version 1.5


max@demo:~$ file archiv
archiv: gzip compressed data, last modified: ...
```

If you want to analyse the content of a device-file like /dev/sda1, you need to use the "-s" commandline switch:

```
max@demo:~$ file /dev/sda1
/dev/sda1: block special
max@demo:~$ sudo file -s /dev/sda1
/dev/sda1: SGI XFS filesystem data (blksz 4096, inosz 512
```

sidenote: because root permissions are needed for reeding the content of /dev/sda, you need to call file via sudo in this example.

stat	get the meta-information of a file and print them out formatted

stat --help
man stat
	With **stat** you can extract any meta-information from a file and print it out formatted as you like.
	
	example: print out the name of a file together with the "human-readable" permissions:
	
	```max@demo:~$ stat archiv -c %n:%A```
	```archiv:-rw-rw-r--```
	
	example: get the modification-time only and print it out as unix-timestamp:
	
	```stat archiv -c %Y```
	```1597917089```

test	check a file for existence and type, check for permissions
test --help help test man test	**test** lets you do a load of checks against a file and sets the returncode ($?) to "0", if the check succeeded. **example:** check if a file exists as a regular file:

```
max@demo:~$ test -f /etc/passwd
max@demo:~$ echo $?
0
```

As you see, the returncode "$?" was set to "0", so our test succeeded. Which means, the file "/etc/passwd" exists.

How about another file?

```
max@demo:~$ test -f /etc/passwd_backup
max@demo:~$ echo $?
1
```

Here you see that "$?" doesn't equal to "0", so the tested name doesn't exist as a regular file.

Is "/root" a directory?

```
max@demo:~$ test -d /root
max@demo:~$ echo $?
0
```

... yes, it is.

Do we have write-permissions there?

```
max@demo:~$ test -w /root
max@demo:~$ echo $?
1
```

And now you: do we?

Hint: As you see - test doesn't give you an output to the command line. Always have a look at `echo $?` after calling **test** to see the resutlt of the test or use the test-command within logical-patterns (if-then-else, while, until, ...).

rm	remove a file
rm --help man rm	To remove one or multiple files, use **rm**.
	Notice, that **rm** by default doesn't ask for confirmation:

```
max@demo:~$ rm archiv
max@demo:~$ rm report1.txt report2.txt
```

if you want to remove an entire directory, use the "-r" switch

```
max@demo:~$ rm -r ~/my_temp_files
```

if you want to suppress all possible warnings and confirmation requests, add "-f".

```
max@demo:~$ rm -rf ~/my_temp_files
```

rmdir	remove a directory
rmdir --help man rmdir	To remove an empty directory, you can use rmdir.

```
rmdir /tmp/pictures
```

Be aware, that rmdir really only removes directories that are empty:

```
max@demo:~$ rmdir /tmp/backup
rmdir: failed to remove '/tmp/backup': Directory not empty
```

exception: a directory that only contains a single empty directory, that contains only a single empty directory, that contains only a single ...

... then you can remove a whole path "reverse" by using the "-p" switch:

```
rmdir -p ~/pictures/2023/summer
```

note: If you want to remove a directory recursively including its content - use rm instead.

tar	work with tar-archives
tar --help man tar	tar-archives are a convenient way to "package" multiple files into one single file (aka the "archive-file").

The "-c" switch stands for "create". The "-f" switch is always followed by the name of the archive-file `tar` shall work with.

The following example creates an archive "archive.tar" with the content coming from "/var/www":

```
tar -c -f archiv.tar /var/www
```

If you want to compress the archive on the fly during creation, use "-z":

```
tar -c -z -f archiv.tar.gz /var/www
```

As nearly always, the command-line options can be written together:

```
tar -czf archiv.tar.gz /var/www
```

To have a look into an archive, use "-t":

```
tar -tzf archiv.tar.gz
```

To extract the content from an archive, use "-x":

```
tar -xzf archiv.tar.gz
```

attention: The content will be extracted into the current directory. To extract the content to a different (existing) directory, add the "-C" switch:

```
tar -tzf archiv.tar.gz -C /tmp
```

gzip	compress and decompress files
gzip --help man gzip	use gzip to replace a file with its compressed version. After compression, the extension ".gz" will be appended to the filename. ```gzip a_large_file``` to decompress the file again, use "gzip -d"

```
gzip -d a_large_file.gz
```

an alternative way would be to use gunzip:

```
gunzip a_large_file.gz
```

gunzip	decompress gzip compressed data
gunzip --help man gunzip	use gunzip to replace a gzip-compressed file with its uncompressed version. After uncompression, the extension ".gz" from the filename will be removed.

```
gunzip a_large_file.gz
```

you can also uncompressed tar-archives:

```
gunzip a_large_archiv.tgz
```

the name of the resulting file in this example would be "a_large_archive.tar"

zcat	just print out the uncompressed content of gzip compressed data
zcat --help man zcat	Sometimes you just want to analyze the content of a compressed text-file. For this, the tool zcat lets you uncompress a file "on-the-fly". **example:** count the lines of a compressed text-file:

```
zcat report.txt.gz | wc -l
```

bzip2	compress and decompress files
bzip2 --help man bzip2	bzip2 works like gzip with a slightly better compression. Filenames compressed with bzip2 have typically the extension

```
bzip2 a_large_file
```

to decompress the file again, use "bzip2 -d":

```
bzip2 -d a_large_file.bz2
```

an alternative way would be to use bunzip2:

```
bunzip2 a_large_file.bz2
```

bunzip2	ecompress bzip2 compressed data
bunzip2 --help man bunzip2	Use bunzip2 to replace a bzip2-compressed file with its uncompressed version. After uncompression, the extension ".bz2" from the filename will be removed. Filenames compressed with bzip2 have typically the extension ".bz2".

```
bunzip2 a_large_file.bz2
```

bzcat	print out the uncompressed content of bzip2 compressed data
bzcat --help man bzcat	Sometimes you just want to analyze the content of a compressed text-file. The tool bzcat lets you uncompress a file "on-the-fly". example: count the lines of a compressed text-file:

```
bzcat report.txt.bz2 | wc -l
```

split	split a file into parts of the same size
split --help man split	split can be used to split a large file into chunks of a given size. This example splits a large file into 1GB parts:

```
split a_very_large_file -b 1G
```

The names of the resulting parts by default look like "xaa", "xab", "xac", …

To concatenate the parts again, you can simply use the `cat` command with an output-redirection:

```
cat x* > a_very_large_file_2
```

dd	print out or read in a file, bytewise or blockwise
dd --help man dd	

dd can be used to print-out a file bytewise or blockwise. Typically this is used to create or write-back disk-images:

example: create an image-file for "/dev/sda1":

```
dd if=/dev/sda1 of=/tmp/sda1.img
```

attention: Make sure /tmp has enough free space to hold the whole image of "/dev/sda1".

write the image back to "/dev/sda1"

```
dd if=/tmp/sda1.img of=/dev/sda1
```

ATTENTION: do this only, if you are sure that the image-file really contains a disk-image.

You can even mirror a disk to another one:

```
dd if=/dev/sda of=/dev/sdb
```

And you can also set the amount of data you want to transfer.

for instance: Make a backup of the MBR ("master boot record") which is 512 Bytes in size:

```
dd if=/dev/sda of=/tmp/mbr.backup bs=512 count=1
```

notice: to read or write from or into the device-files for the disks, you typically need to be root (eg. use `sudo`).

grep	search for lines within a file containing a search-pattern
grep --help man grep	grep works line-based and prints per default every line containing a given pattern:

```
max@demo:~$ grep root /etc/passwd
root:x:0:0:root:/root:/bin/bash
```

the search-pattern can be a regular expression:

```
max@demo:~$ grep "^r..t:" /etc/passwd
root:x:0:0:root:/root:/bin/bash
```

if you only want to count the lines containing a pattern, use "-c":

```
max@demo:~$ grep -c bash /etc/passwd
8
```

find	search for files recursively by a given criteria
find --help man find	find searches recursively the given directory (or the current directory) for files matching the given criteria.

example: search for files in /etc/ which names containing "pass"

```
find /etc -name "*pass*"
```

example: search in /tmp for symbolic-links older than 7 days

```
find /tmp -type l -mtime +7
```

sed	search and replace patterns within a file
sed --help man sed	Though sed is a "stream editor" for modifying datastreams, it can be used very easily to find and replace patterns within a file.

To do this, you have to use the "substitution-mode" of sed by giving a parameter in the following format:

s/OLD-PATTERN/NEW-PATTERN/g

sed will then take the content of the file and replace each occurence of "OLD-PATTERN" with "NEW-PATTERN".

By default, the result will only be printed out and the original-content of the file won't be touched:

```
sed 's/root/administrator/g' /etc/passwd
```

This will replace every occurence of the word "root" with "administrator" and the result will be printed out.

If you want to replace directly within a file, add the "-i" switch:

```
sed -i 's/max/robert/g' report.txt
```

attention: Please double-check your command line, before destroying important data.

md5sum	generate a md5-hash as a fingerprint for the content of a file
md5sum --help man md5sum	By calculating the checksum for the content of a file, you can tell if two files have identical content or if a file was modified since you calculated the checksum last time.

As the name implies, md5sum uses the hash function "MD5" for checksum calculation.

example: compare the checksum of "/etc/passwd" with the checksum of a previously generated copy of this file:

```
max@demo:~$ md5sum /etc/passwd
8d1d2a424b98f724a644b1df5a74d92a  /etc/passwd
max@demo:~$ md5sum /tmp/passwd_copy
8d1d2a424b98f724a644b1df5a74d92a  /tmp/passwd_copy
```

sha1sum	generate a sha1-hash as a fingerprint for the content of a file
sha1sum --help man sha1sum	By calculating the checksum for the content of a file, you can tell if two files have identical content or if a file was modified since you calculated the checksum last time.

As the name implies, `sha1sum` uses the hash function "SHA1" for checksum calculation.

example: compare the checksum of "/etc/passwd" with the checksum of a previously generated copy of this file:

```
max@demo:~$ sha1sum /etc/passwd
ff475d1cc30b197c03482c2a865ef37740c0e317  /etc/passwd
max@demo:~$ sha1sum /tmp/passwd_copy
ff475d1cc30b197c03482c2a865ef37740c0e317  /tmp/passwd_copy
```

Disks & Filesystems

If you want to mount additional disks or create new partitions and filesystems - here are the needed tools. Keep in mind that most of the tools here need root-permissions (directly or via `sudo`).

mount	mount an existing filesystem into the directory-tree

mount --help
 man mount
	`mount` can be used to mount an existing filesystem - typically a disk-partition or removable storage-device - into the current directory tree.
	
	 In the most simple case, you give two parameters to the `mount` command: the device file that should be mounted and a (empty) directory as the mountpoint.
	
	 example: mount the partition "/dev/sdb1" to "/mnt"
	
	 `mount /dev/sdb1 /mnt`
	
	 example: mount the cdrom (linked to by "/dev/cdrom") to "/media/cdrom"
	
	 `mount /dev/cdrom /media/cdrom`
	
	 `mount` can also be used to mount network-based filesystems like NFS or CIFS
	
	 example: mount an NFS-share
	
	 `mount 10.10.2.3:/export /srv/data`
	
	 if you need to apply mount-options, use the "-o" switch for this.
	
	 example: mount a CIFS-share read-only
	
	 `mount -o ro //fileserver/export /srv/www`
	
	 Filesystems that should be mounted by default while the system-boots, need to be configured within the file "/etc/fstab" (see `man 5 fstab` for a documentation)

If you add a filesystem to "/etc/fstab" for an automatic mount, you can use "-a" for the mount-command to mount the missing filesystem without a reboot:

```
mount -a
```

notice: If you want to see all the mounted filesystems, call mount without an argument.

umount	unmount a filesystem
umount --help man umount	To unlink a mounted filesystem from the global directory-tree, use umount. umount takes either the mount-point or the device-file you want to unmount as a parameter. **example:** Unmount a filesystem that is currently mounted to "/media/cdrom":

```
umount /media/cdrom
```

notice: only filesystems that are not in use can be unmounted. If the filesystem is in use, you'll get an "device or resource busy" error. If you need, you can use lsof to examine the opened files.

lsof	list open files
lsof --help man lsof	lsof gives you a list of all open files on the system.

```
lsof
```

As lsof gives a list of really all open files (this includes filesystem sockets and even network sockets), it can be useful to filter the output with grep.

```
lsof | grep /media/cdrom
```

If you are interested only in open files under a given path, give this path to lsof as a single parameter:

```
lsof /media/cdrom
```

fdisk	show, create or manage partitions on a disk

fdisk --help
man fdisk
	fdisk is used to show or manage partitions on block-devices (aka disks).
	
	fdisk can give you an overview over all available partitions:
	
	```fdisk -l```
	
	or all partitions on a given disk
	
	```fdisk -l /dev/sda```
	
	to manage the partitions on a disk, omit the "-l" switch:
	
	```fdisk /dev/sda```
	
	Now you need to follow the instructions within the interactive fdisk command. Use for instance "m" to get help.
	
	note: fdisk typically needs root-permissions (sudo)

partprobe	let the kernel update the meta-data for available partitions
partprobe --help man partprobe	After creating a new partition or modifying an existing one, it may be necessary to let the kernel reread its known partition information to avoid the reboot of the system: ```partprobe```

mkfs	create a filesystem on a block-device
mkfs --help man mkfs	mkfs is the tool to create a filesystem on a block-device:

```
mkfs /dev/sdb1
```

If you want to specify explicitly the type of the filesystem to be created, call mkfs with the "-t" switch followed by the filesystem-type:

```
mkfs -t ext4 /dev/sdb1
```

Because mkfs doesn't know anything about filesystems, it simply calls a filesystem-specific tool for doing the hard work. These tools are named after the filesystem they are used for - "mkfs."

If you want, you can call these commands directly:

```
mkfs.ext4 /dev/sdb1
```

It's also useful to know these background-commands, if you need some documentation for creating a specific filesystem:

```
man mkfs.ext4
```

important notice: You are seldomly asked for confirmation before a filesystem is created and potentially existing data on the target disk are destroyed.

fsck	do a filesystem-check
fsck --help man fsck	If you assume an error with the integrity of a filesystem, you can try to solve it with a filesystem-check:

```
fsck /dev/sdb1
```

notice: to avoid data data-corruption, the filesystem has typically to be unmounted.

Just like mkfs, fsck redirects the real work to tools named after the filesystem-type - for instance fsck.ext4.

So if you want to do filesystem-specific operations or you want to force a check for a seemingly clean filesystem, have a look at the documentation of these filesystem-specific tools:

```
man fsck.ext4
```

df	show the used disk-space for all mounted filesystems

df --help
man df

Use df to see all currently mounted filesystems and their fill-level:

```
max@demo:~$ df
Filesystem      1K-blocks      Used Available Use% Mounted oi
/dev/xvda1      24638844 2732756   20647848  12% /
udev              494380        4     494376   1% /dev
tmpfs             201528      276     201252   1% /run
```

If you want to see the used and free disk-space in a more "human readable" format instead of "blocks", use the "-h" switch for the "human readable" format:

```
max@demo:~$ df -h
Filesystem      Size  Used Avail Use% Mounted on
/dev/xvda1       24G  2.7G   20G  12% /
udev            483M  4.0K  483M   1% /dev
tmpfs           197M  276K  197M   1% /run
```

For some types of filesystems, the filesystem can run out of inodes before running out of data blocks. To see the fill-level for the inodes, use "-i":

```
max@demo:~$  df -i
Filesystem       Inodes  IUsed    IFree IUse% Mounted on
/dev/xvda1      1572864 111355  1461509    8% /
udev             123595    458   123137    1% /dev
tmpfs            125953    358   125595    1% /run
```

file	get the type of a filesystem on a block-device

file --help
man file

The tool file is the tool the tries to give you the type of every-file you give it as a parameter:

```
max@demo:~$ file /dev/sda1
/deb/sda1: block special (8/2)
```

If you now add the "-s" switch to the command line and call "file" as root, then file will open the device-file for reading and tries to interpret the filesystem it sees:

```
max@demo:~$ sudo file -s /dev/sda1
/dev/sdb1: Linux rev 1.0 ext4 filesystem data, ...
```

Datastream Operations

Here I have compiled a collection of tools for working with datastreams.

If you have a command that prints out some data - then this is a datastream. The tools in this chapter help you modify the content of these datastreams or to extract needed data.

echo	generate a datastream

echo --help
help echo
man echo
	echo is the most simple tool to print something out to the console - and therefore it lets you generate a datastream in a simple way:
	
	```echo "Hello World"```
	
	to suppress the newline echo adds to every output, use the "-n" switch:
	
	```echo -n "Hello "; echo -n "World";```
	
	If you want to print out special characters like tabs or line breaks, you can use the "-e" command-line switch:
	
	```echo -e "Hello\tWorld\nnew line"```
	
	In combination with the output-redirection, echo can also be used to generate a datastream for the error-output "stderr"
	
	```echo "this shall be an error message" 1>&2```

cat	print the input-datastream while marking special characters
cat --help man cat	cat can be used, if the datastream you want to create shall contain the content of a file: ```cat /etc/passwd``` If you don't give a filename, cat simply prints out the data it gets via stdin. Within datastreams, cat is often used to mark special characters like TABs, NEWLINEs or other.

To mark all recognized special characters, use the "-A" switch:

```
echo -e "Hello\tWorld" | cat -A
```

tac	print the input-datastream while reversing the lines
tac --help man tac	Just like `cat`, `tac` prints out a file or the data it gets via stdin to its output-datastream.

But unlike `cat`, `tac` reverses the order of the lines before printing them out.

example: print out the lines of "/etc/passwd" in reverse order:

```
tac /etc/profile
```

example: reverse the lines of a given datastream

```
max@demo:~$ echo -e "first line\nsecond line" | tac
second line
first line
```

If needed, `tac` can also reverse the datastream not linewise but at a different separator than a newline:

```
echo "Hello World" | tac -s " "
```

cut	cut lines from a datastream into parts at a given delimiter
cut --help man cut	`cut` lets you extract one or multiple fields from a datastream, if the fields in the lines are separable by a single character or tab.

With "-d" you set the delimiter (if not a TAB) and with "-f" the fields you want to extract.

Example: Extract only the username (field 1) and the login-shell (field 7) from the datastream generated from /etc/passwd:

```
cat /etc/passwd | cut -d : -f 1,7
```

head	print out only the first lines of a datastream
head --help man head	head is the tool, that gives you only the first lines of a datastream. The number of lines to show defaults defaults to 10.

```
ps ax | head
```

To set the number of lines you want to get, use the "-n" switch followed by the number.

example: show only the first 3 line of the output from "ps ax":

```
max@demo:~$ ps ax | head -n 3
  PID TTY      STAT   TIME COMMAND
    1 ?        Ss     0:01 /usr/lib/systemd/systemd --swi
    2 ?        S      0:00 [kthreadd]
```

tail	print out only the last lines of a datastream
tail --help man tail	Sometimes you don't need a whole datastream but only the last lines. By using `tail`, you'll get by default the last 10 lines:

```
ls -l /etc | tail
```

If you want to, you can set the number of lines you want to see with the "-n" switch:

example: get the smalles file within the current directory ("ls -S" sorts by size):

```
ls -S | tail -n 1
```

grep	search for lines within a datastream containing a search-pattern
grep --help man grep	grep is the tool to search*within* files or datastreams. And it can perfectly be used to filter the output of a command:

```
max@demo:~$ ps ax | grep bash
435 pts/0   S<    0:00 bash --login
```

grep by default works linewise and prints out only the lines containing the search-pattern.

the search-pattern can be a regular expression:

```
max@demo:~$ getent passwd | grep "^r..t:"
root:x:0:0:root:/root:/bin/bash
```

if you only want to count the lines containing a pattern, use "-c":

```
max@demo:~$ getent passwd | grep -c "^r..t:"
1
```

if you only want to see lines *not* containing the search-pattern, negate the search-pattern with "-v":

```
max@demo:~$ getent passwd | grep -c -v bash
28
```

read	read one single line from the input-datastream into a variable
read --help help read	read can be used to read in one single line (the first one) from the input-datastream into a variable:

```
getent passwd | (read LINE; echo "line: $LINE")
```

sort	sort the input-datastream
sort --help man sort	If you want to sort something, then **sort** is *the tool* for you.

The flexibility of sort lets you sort data in nearly every way possible.

example: sort the output of "getent passwd" alphabetically:

```
getent passwd | sort
```

example: sort the output of "du" numerically:

```
du -s * | sort -n
```

example: sort the output of "du -h" based on the human-readable format:

```
du -sh * | sort -h
```

example: sort the content of /etc/passwd numerically by the UID (the 3rd field in every line):

The field-separator is given via "-t" and the field to sort on with "-k":

```
cat /etc/passwd | sort -t : -k 3 -n
```

As with many other tools here, sort be used directly with a filename as a parameter to use the content of this file as input-datastream:

```
sort -t : -k 3 -n /etc/passwd
```

uniq	remove or identify duplicates in the sorted input-datastream

uniq --help
man uniq
	`uniq` lets you remove or find duplicates in a pre-sorted datastream.
	
	To show all duplicates in a datastream, use the "-D" switch.
	
	example: determine if there are duplicate lines in the file "names.txt" and print them out:
	
	```cat names.txt | sort | uniq -D```
	
	Do you notice the use of **sort** in front of **uniq**? As mentioned already, **uniq** needs a presorted datastream to work.
	
	If there are duplicates, you can remove them simply from the stream:
	
	```cat names.txt | sort | uniq```
	
	The last example this time without the **cat** command for illustration:
	
	```sort names.txt | uniq```

tr	substitute or delete single characters on the input-datastream
tr --help man tr	**tr** is a tool that lets you substitute single characters - just as if you want to "translate" them

Substitute characters by simply give two parameters to **tr** as a "substitution table".

For substituting only one single character, both parameters contain only one character.

example: replace every "l" with an "f":

```
max@demo:~$ echo "Hello World" | tr l f
Heffo Worfd
```

To substitute two characters at ones, add a second substitution to the "table":

```
max@demo:~$ echo "Hello World" | tr le fU
HUffo Worfd
```

The same with a third one (and so on).

If you need, you can give ranges within the substitution parameters.

example: replace all lowercase characters with uppercase characters:

```
max@demo:~$ echo "Hello World" | tr a-z A-Z
HELLO WORLD
```

Sometimes it is useful to remove unwanted characters from a datastream. Use **tr** for this with the "-d" switch:

```
max@demo:~$ echo "Hello World" | tr -d eo
Hll Wrld
```

Or you can "squeeze" repeating characters with "-s":

```
max@demo:~$ echo "Hello World" | tr -s l
Helo World
```

wc	count the lines, words or characters of the input-datastream
wc --help man wc	The name "wc" stands for "word count" and it lets you count the words, lines and characters or even bytes of a file (or a datastream). How many users are known on the system? ``` getent passwd | wc -l ``` How many characters are within a string? ``` echo "Hello World" | wc -c ```

rev	reverse the characters of each input-line
rev --help man rev	With rev you can reverse the input-datastream characterwise: ``` max@demo:~$ echo "Hello World" | rev dlroW olleH ```

tee	print out the input-datastream while logging it into a file
tee --help man tee	tee is a great tool, if you need to spread a datastream to two or more destinations. tee reads its input from the input-datastream ("stdin"). One destination for the output is always the output-datastream "stdout", all additional copies of the datastream go to the files you specify as parameters: ``` max@demo:~$ echo "Hello World" | tee file1 file2 Hello World ```

xargs	convert the input-datastream to command-line parameters
xargs --help man xargs	Sometime you need to connect a datastream to a tool that doesn't read from "stdin". Then you typically need xargs to "convert" the input-datastream to command-line parameters.

example: feed some filenames to the input datastream ("stdin") of xargs, that in turn then calls rm with these filenames as command-line parameters:

```
echo file1 file2 file3 | xargs rm
```

In this example, xargs calls rm exactly once and gives it everything it reads via its input-datastream.

For splitting the datastream into single parameters, xargs splits the datastream by default at whitespaces, tabs and newlines.

Sometimes you want to process every parameter on its own. This could be done by specifying a "replace-string" that will be substituted at the command line with one single parameter:

example: copy all files to /tmp

```
ls | xargs -I FILE cp -pr FILE /tmp
```

Here "-I FILE" sets the replace-string to "FILE" which then can be used at the command line for cp.

sed	print out the edited/modified input-datastream
sed --help man sed	As sed stands for "stream editor", it can be used to modify datastreams "on-the-fly" and print out the result as a new datastream.

An often seen usecase is to replace words or strings within a datastream.

To do this, you have to use the "substitution-mode" of sed by giving a parameter in the following format:

s/OLD-PATTERN/NEW-PATTERN/g

sed will then read in its input-datastream and replace each occurrence of "OLD-PATTERN" with "NEW-PATTERN".

example: Replace every occurrence of the word "World" with "Max" and print out the resulting datastream:

```
max@demo:~$ echo "Hello World" | sed 's/World/Max/g'
Hello Max
```

If you need to, you can do multiple substitutions at once. Simply give multiple substitution patterns prepended with the switch "-e":

```
cat /etc/passwd | sed -e 's/root/ROOT/g' -e 's/bash/sh/g'
```

awk	print out certain fields from the input-datastream
awk --help man awk	Although awk is a complete programming language on its own, it can relatively simply be used at the command line for extracting columns from a datastream. If you want to extract data from lines, where the fields are organized as columns separated by one or more whitespaces/tabs, then awk can be used directly to extract single or multiple columns:

```
max@demo:~$ echo "these    are some    columns" | awk '{pr
some
```

awk-commands are written within curly brackets "{ ... }" and the print-command is used for printing something out. With $1,$2,$3, ... you can reference the columns you are interested in.

example: use **df** to show the used disk space of all partitions but print only the mount-point and the percentage separated by a colon:

```
df | awk '{print $6 ":" $5}'
```

Searching

Not many but very powerful tools can be used for searching on a system. Have a look for the tools for searching for files and for searching within files or datastreams.

which	search for an executable file within the search-path $PATH
which --help man which	**which** shows you the binary that the shell would execute, if you would call a command with a given name. **example:** Which binary will be started if we simply use "passwd" as command? ```max@demo:~$ which passwd /usr/bin/passwd``` to be exact: **which** searches every directory from the search-path ($PATH) from start till the end, until it finds an executable file with the given name.

grep	search for lines within a file or a datastream

grep --help
man grep
	grep is the tool to search*within* files or datastreams.
	
	grep takes as an argument the pattern it shall search for. It then
	
	If you call grep with a filename as a parameter, then grep reads in and searches the content of a file:
	
	``max@demo:~$ grep root /etc/passwd
	root:x:0:0:root:/root:/bin/bash```
	
	If you omit the name of a file, then grep reads from its input-datastream stdin and searches there:
	
	``max@demo:~$ ps ax
		grep bash
		435 pts/0 S< 0:00 bash --login```
		
		the search-pattern can be e regular expression:

```
max@demo:~$ grep "^r..t:" /etc/passwd
root:x:0:0:root:/root:/bin/bash
```

if you only want to count the lines containing a pattern, use "-c":

```
max@demo:~$ grep -c bash /etc/passwd
8
```

if you only want to see lines *not* containing the search-pattern, negate the search-pattern with "-v":

```
max@demo:~$ grep -c -v bash /etc/passwd
28
```

If you want to, you can also use grep to recursively search within all files within a directory. Use the "-r" switch for this:

```
grep -r max /etc
```

find	search for files recursively by a given criteria
find --help man find	find searches recursively the given directory (or the current directory) for files matching the given criteria.

example: search for files in /etc/ which names containing "pass"

```
find /etc -name "*pass*"
```

example: search in /tmp for symbolic-links older than 7 days

```
find /tmp -type l -mtime +7
```

Users & Groups

In this chapter I collected the tools you'll use for the typical user-management. Needless to say, that most of the tools that modify the user-database have to be run as root (or via sudo).

getent	get or filter for all known users or groups on a system

getent --help
man getent
	getent prints out system-databases reachable via the "Name Service Switch" libraries (NSS).
	
	It can perfectly be used to list all users that are known to the system - not only those configured locally via /etc/passwd:
	
	`getent passwd`
	
	to get a list of known groups, ask for the "group" database:
	
	`getent group`
	
	notice: Sometimes remote user directories aren't configured for enumeration of all available users. In this case `getent passwd` or `getent group` will give you only a list of the locally defined users.
	
	Nethertheless, you can always retrieve the information from a single specified user or group.
	
	You do this, by giving the name of the user or group as second commandline parameter to getent:
	
	`getent passwd max`
	`max:x:1014:1014:Max:/home/max:/bin/bash`

useradd	create a new user
useradd --help man useradd	With `useradd` you can create add a new user - fast and simple: `useradd -m max` The command-line switch "-m" is used here to force the `useradd` tool to create a home-directory for the new user.

To force a defined loginshell for the user, use the "-s" switch. For setting the comment-field (aka the "realname" or the "gecos"-field), use -c:

```
useradd -m -s /bin/bash -c "Max Smith" max
```

usermod	modify an existing user
usermod --help man usermod	With usermod, you can change the properties of an existing user. example: change the login-shell of the user "max" to the korn-shell ("/bin/ksh") ```usermod -s /bin/ksh max```

userdel	remove a user from the system

userdel --help
man userdel
	To remove a user, simply use userdel:
	
	```userdel max```
	
	If you want to remove the home-directory while removing the user, add the "-r" switch:
	
	```userdel -r max```

passwd	set or change the password of a user
passwd --help man passwd	passwd lets you change your own password or the password of a named user. example: change the password of the user "max": ```passwd max``` if you want to change your own password, simply call passwd without any argument. passwd can also be used to "lock" a user:

```
passwd -l max
```

A locked-user cannot login anymore until he is unlocked again.

to unlock the user:

```
passwd -u max
```

notice: This command has to be run as root (or via **sudo**) unless you want to change the password of the currently active user (aka your user).

chage	get or modify information about the password-age

chage --help
man chage
	The file "/etc/shadow" contains beside the hashed password also expire-information about the password or the whole account. To easily read and set this information without the need to modify
	
	example: list the current expire-information of the user max
	
	```chage -l max```
	
	example: set the maximum number of days for which a password is valid to 90 days:
	
	```chage -M 90 max```

groupadd	create a new group
groupadd --help man groupadd	this simply creates a new group: ```groupadd testers```

groupmod	modify an existing group
| groupmod --help<br>man groupmod | to modify an existing group, user groupmod<br><br>**example:** rename a group<br><br>```
groupmod -n web-testers testers
``` |

groupdel	remove a group from the system
| groupdel --help<br>man groupdel | as the name says, groupdel lets you remove an existing group from the system. You can remove any group that is not the primary-group of a user.<br><br>```
groupdel web-testers
``` |

id	show the UID and the groups-memberships of a user
| id --help<br>man id | Show the user-id (UID) and the group-memberships of a user:<br><br>```
max@demo:~$ id root
uid=0(root) gid=0(root) groups=0(root)
```<br><br>If you omit the username, **id** gives you the same information for the current user:<br><br>```
max@demo:~$ id
uid=1001(max) gid=1001(max) groups=1001(max),27(sudo)
``` |

whoami	shows the name of the user owning the current shell
| whoami --help<br>man whoami | prints out the username currently active in the shell.<br><br>```
max@demo:~$ whoami
max
``` |
```

w	show all currently logged-in users
w --help man w	w gives you a list of all currently logged in users and what they are doing currently. The output in the following example might be truncated due to space restrictions:

```
max@demo:~$ w
 09:06:07 up 72 days,  1:36,  1 user,  load average:
 USER     TTY       FROM             LOGIN@   IDLE   JCPU
 max      pts/0     34.90.189.110    08:39    1.00s  0.03s
 root     tty0      -                09:17    12mins 0.07s
```

who	show all currently logged in users
who --help man who	The command who is another way to list the currently logged in users. The output-format differs from the output of "w":

```
max@demo:~$ who
root     tty0           2024-04-29 09:17
max      pts/0          2024-04-29 08:39 (34.90.189.110)
```

Filesystem Permissions

If you master the user-base of your system, then the next step is to control what each user can do. For this, here are to tools for the permission-management:

test	test the permissions the current user has for a file
help test man test	In the context of filesystem permissioins, the command **test** lets you check your permission-level against a file. **Hint:** always have a look at "echo $?" after calling **test** to see the result of the test. Or use the test-command within logical-patterns (if-then-else, while, until, ...) Do we have read permissions for the file /etc/passwd? ``` max@demo:~$ test -r /etc/passwd max@demo:~$ echo $? 0 ``` The returncode is "0" - so we have. Do we have write-permissions? ``` max@demo:~$ test -w /etc/passwd max@demo:~$ echo $? 1 ``` The returncode is different from "0" - so we don't.

chown	change the owner of a file
chown --help man chown	Every file on the system is owned by exactly one single user. Typically this is the user who created the file. If you have root-permissions, then you can use **chown** to change the owning user of a file later on: ``` chown max report.txt ``` Sometimes it can be handy, to change also the owning-group at the same time:

```
chown max:web-testers report.txt
```

or you can even change only the group via chown:

```
chown :web-testers report.txt
```

chgrp	change the owning-group of a file
chgrp --help man chgrp	Every file on the system belongs to exactly one single group. This is typically the effective group of the user who created the file at the time where he created it.

If you have root permissions, you can use chgrp to change this owning group:

```
chgrp web-testers report.txt
```

You can also change the owning group, if you are the owner of the file *and* you are a member of the new owning group.

chmod	change the permissions of a file
chmod --help man chmod	chmod is the tool that lets you change the permissions of a file.

You can use chmod in a symbolic- and in a numeric way.

example for symbolic: give others read-permissions

```
chmod o+r report.txt
```

example for numeric: only the owner shall have read- and write-access

```
chmod 600 report.txt
```

getfacl	get the acls set for a file
getfacl --help man getfacl	Posix-ACLs are a convenient way on modern Linux systems, to give permissions to a list of users or groups. with getfacl you can get the currently valid ACLs for a file ``` getfacl report.txt ``` **notice:** if getfacl isn't available as a command, you have to install the "acl" or "acl-tools" package.

setfacl	modify the acl of a file
setfacl --help man setfacl	Posix-ACLs are a convenient way on modern Linux systems, to give permissions to a list of users or groups. With **setfacl** you can modify the currently valid ACL for a file. **example:** add read/write-permissions for "max" to a file: ``` setfacl -m user:max:rw report.txt ``` **example:** remove the ACL based permissions for the group "web-testers": ``` setfacl -x group:web-testers report.txt ``` **notice:** if setfacl isn't available as a command, you have to install the "acl" or "acl-tools" package.

Process Management

What processes are running on a system? How to control them? See the tools in this chapter:

ps	get a list of all running processes

ps --help
man ps
	ps gives you a list of currently running processes.
	
	If you call ps without any command-line switches, you'll see only the processes that are running in your current terminal.
	
	If you want to see all your running processes, regardless of the terminal, use the switch "x" (yes - without the leading dash):
	
	`ps x`
	
	If you want to see *all* running processes (also the processes from other user-contexts), add "a":
	
	`ps ax`
	
	Do you also want to see the user-context a process is running in? Add as a third switch the "u":
	
	`ps aux`

pstree	get a list of running processes with parent-child dependencies

pstree --help
man pstree
	Every process - beside the process with the PID 1 - has a parent-process it depends on.
	
	To see all processes on a system together with all parent-child-dependencies, use pstree:
	
	`pstree`
	
	A common command-line switch for pstree is "-p" which gives you additionally the PID of each running process:
	
	`pstree -p`

top	get a dynamically updated and sorted list of running processes
top --help man top	top gives you a dynamically sorted list of all running processes and some useful information about the current state of the system:

```
top
```

The list of processes is by default sorted by the cpu-load each process produces and is updated every two seconds:

```
top - 08:38:29 up  1:32,  0 users,  load average: 0.04, 0
Tasks: 120 total,   1 running,  77 sleeping,   0 stopped,
%Cpu(s):  0.5 us,  0.8 sy,  0.0 ni, 98.5 id,  0.0 wa,  0.0
KiB Mem :   970908 total,   211932 free,   533432 used,
KiB Swap:  2047996 total,  1971964 free,    76032 used.

  PID USER      PR  NI    VIRT    RES    SHR S  %CPU %MEM
 4122 root      20   0 1700976  14396   2376 S   0.7  1.5
 3136 root      20   0 1383424  18168   5404 S   0.3  1.9
```

You can end the top command by simply hitting "q" for "quit".

While top is running, you can for instance change the sorting to memory consumption by hittin "M" (the uppercase "m").

top can also be used in "batch-mode", where it prints out the sorted process-list to the console ("stdout") for further processing:

```
top -b -n 1
```

kill	send a signal to or terminate a process identified by its PID
kill --help man kill	With the command kill you can "kill" a process - that means you can terminate it.

The command to terminate has to be addressed by its process-id (PID):

```
kill 123
```

If you call kill in this way, kill simply sends the signal 15 (aka the signal "SIGTERM") to the process with the PID 123. Typically this process will terminate as a result.

To send a different signal than SIGTERM, add "-SIGNAL" as a parameter.

send signal 9 ("SIGKILL"):

```
kill -9 123
```

you can also address a signal by its name:

```
kill -KILL 123
```

To see a list of all defined signals, use the "-l" switch.

```
kill -l
```

notice: you need to be root or the owner of a process to send it a signal.

killall	send a signal to or terminate a process identified by its name

killall --help
man killall
	killall works like the command kill with the difference, that you don't address a process by its PID but by its name:
	
	```killall apache2```
	
	Like with the kill command, by default a SIGTERM (15) is sent to all processes with the given name.
	
	If needed, give the signal that shall be send:
	
	```killall -HUP apache2```

wait	wait for a background-process to terminate
wait --help help wait	The command wait is mostly used within scripts or automations. If you start a command in the background (with "&" appended), then To wait later on for the termination of this process, simply call "wait" with this PID as a parameter:

```
max@demo:~$ sleep 100 &
[1] 4520
max@demo:~$ echo $!
4520
max@demo:~$ wait 4520 # now we have to be patient ...
[1]+  Done                    sleep 100
```

nice	start a process with a modified priority
nice --help man nice	By default all processes you start on a system are running with the same priority. If you want to have a process with a different priority, then you need to start it with a different nice-level. The default nice-level is 0 and it can range from -20 (very high priority) to +19 (very low priority). To start a process with a priority other than the default, use nice with the switch "-<nice-level>" and the command line you want to run: `nice -n 19 gzip /tmp/very_huge_file` notice: a nice-level < 0 can only be set by root.

renice	change the priority of a running process
renice --help man renice	If you want to change the nice-level (and with it the priority) of a running process, use `renice`. Give the nice-level as the first parameter, the PID of the process as the second one. example: change the nice-level of the running process with the PID "1234" to the value "10". `renice 10 1234` notice: reducing the nice-level can only be done by root.

service	control services on most Linux-distributions

service --help
man service
	The command **service** can be used to start or stop a service on the system.
	
	Though this command was originally implemented for controlling System-V start/stop-scripts in "/etc/init.d", it can also be used to control services managed via systemd.
	
	example: start the service postfix:
	
	`service postfix start`
	
	example: stop the service postfix:
	
	`service postfix restart`
	
	The following actions are typically implemented:
	
	• **start** ... start a service
	• **stop** ... stop a service
	• **restart** ... restart a service
	• **status** ... get the status of a service
	• **reload** ... reload the configuration of a service without terminating the processes

systemctl	control services on a systemd based Linux system

systemctl --help
man systemctl
	systemctl is the tool for controlling services managed by systemd.
	
	example: start the service postfix:
	
	`systemctl start postfix`
	
	example: get the current status of the service postfix:
	
	`systemctl status postfix`
	
	the following actions are typically implemented:
	
	• **start** ... start a service
	• **stop** ... stop a service

- **restart** ... restart a service
- **status** ... get the status of a service
- **reload** ... reload the configuration of a service without terminating the processes

journalctl	read the logs on systemd-based systems
journalctl --help man journalctl	On systemd-based systems (all modern Linux distributions) is an additional logging-service available: the "systemd-journald". `journalctl` lets you read and filter the system-logs in a really flexible way. get all available log-messages:

```
journalctl
```

filter the log-messages with grep, searching only for lines containing "FAILED":

```
journalctl | grep "FAILED"
```

show only log-messages between 8am and 2pm:

```
journalctl --since 08:00 --until 14:00
```

show only log regarding the services "postfix" and "crond"

```
journalctl -u postfix -u crond
```

Software Management

I originally left that chapter about software management out. Just because the tools for software management differ between Linux distributions and sometimes even between distribution-versions. So if you want to use these tools - simply check which one is available on your system.

Software management for Debian based systems

On debian based systems (like debian itself, ubuntu, Linux Mint, Kali Linux, etc.) software-packages are distributed as "*.deb" files.

For an overview of Debian based Linux distributions have a look at wikipedia for instance [https://en.wikipedia.org/wiki/Category:Debian-based_distributions]

dpkg	manage single debian software-packages

dpkg --help
man dpkg
	get a list of all installed software-packages:
	
	`dpkg -l`
	
	install a software-package from the file "software-1.1.1.deb" (or replace a previous installed version of the same package):
	
	`dpkg -i software-1.1.1.deb`
	
	remove an installed package with the name "mypackage":
	
	`dpkg -r mypackage`
	
	list all files contained in an installed package named "mypackage":
	
	`dpkg -L mypackage`
	
	note: for many operations root-permissions are required (**sudo**).

apt-get	manage software-packages and dependencies via repositories
apt-get --help man apt-get	Available software repositories for the APT-system are configured in /etc/apt/sources.list or single files in /etc/apt/sources.list.d/

install the package "postfix" including all needed dependencies:

```
apt-get install postfix
```

to later upgrade a package to a newer version, simply run the install again.

update the local list of known software-packages and versions from the online-repositories (aka "search for updates"):

```
apt-get update
```

install the newest version of all currently installed packages:

```
apt-get upgrade
```

remove (uninstall) the installed package "postfix":

```
apt-get remove postfix
```

remove all automatically installed packages that are no longer needed:

```
apt-get autoremove
```

note: for many operations root-permissions are required (sudo).

apt-cache	query the local copy of repository data
apt-cache --help man apt-cache	do a full text search on all available packages for the phrase "postfix":

```
apt-cache search postfix
```

show all dependencies of the package named "postfix":

```
apt-cache depends postfix
```

show information about the available package "postfix":

```
apt-cache show postfix
```

apt	a higher level interface for apt-get and apt-cache
apt --help man apt	The often used arguments of `apt-get` and `apt-cache` can be used with apt too.

Search for an available software-package by the phrase "postfix":

```
apt search postfix
```

install a package with the name "postfix":

```
apt install postfix
```

remove an installed package named "postfix":

```
apt remove postfix
```

remove all automatically installed packages that are no longer needed:

```
apt autoremove
```

Software management for RPM based systems

On RPM based systems (like Red Hat Enterprise Linux, Fedora, Mandriva and SUSE Linux) software-packages are distributed as "*.rpm" files.

For an overview of RPM based Linux distributions have a look at wikipedia for instance [https://en.wikipedia.org/wiki/Category:RPM-based_Linux_distributions]

rpm	anage single rpm software-packages
rpm --help man rpm	rpm is the "low-level" tool for the software-management on rpm-based distributions like **RedHat**, **SuSE** and **Amazon Linux**. **example:** install a software-package from the file "software-1.1.1.rpm": <code>rpm -i software-1.1.1.rpm</code> **example:** upgrade a software-package from the file "software-2.0.rpm": <code>rpm -U software-2.0.rpm</code> Note the uppercase "-U" command-line switch. The same command line can be used for installing a new software-package. **example:** list all installed software-packages: <code>rpm -qa</code> **example:** get a list of all files contained in the installed software-package "postfix": <code>rpm -ql postfix</code> **example:** get a list of all files contained in the rpm-file "software-1.1.1.rpm": <code>rpm -qlp software-1.1.1.rpm</code>

yum	Software-Management via repositories
yum --help man yum	**yum** is a software-management tool often seen for instance on **RedHat** or **Amazon Linux**. Available software-repositories are configured in single ".repo"-files in "/etc/yum.repos.d/". **example:** search for available software-packages in all connected repositories based on the search-phrase "httpd":

```
yum search httpd
```

example: install the software-package "httpd" including all needed dependencies:

```
yum install httpd
```

example: remove the installed package "httpd":

```
yum remove httpd
```

example: remove all automatically installed but no longer needed packages:

```
yum autoremove
```

example: update all installed packages to the latest available version:

```
yum update
```

dnf	Software-Management via repositories
dnf --help man dnf	**dnf** is the "next-generation" version of **yum** and is used for instance in **Fedora** (since version 22) and **Red Hat Enterprise Linux** (since version 8). Available software-repositories are configured in single ".repo"-files in "/etc/yum.repos.d/".

example: search for available software-packages in all connected repositories based on the search-phrase "httpd":

```
dnf search httpd
```

example: install the software-package "httpd" including all needed dependencies:

```
dnf install httpd
```

example: remove the installed package "httpd":

```
dnf remove httpd
```

note: no longer needed dependencies are automatically removed.

example: remove all automatically installed but no longer needed packages:

```
dnf autoremove
```

example: update all installed packages to the latest available version:

```
dnf update
```

zypper	Software-Management via repositories
zypper --help man zypper	zypper is a software-management tool often seen on **SUSE Linux**. Available software-repositories are configured in single ".repo"-files in "/etc/zypp/repos.d/". **example:** search for available software-packages in all connected repositories based on the search-phrase "apache2": `zypper search apache2` **example:** install the software-package "apache2" including all needed dependencies:

```
zypper install apache2
```

example: remove the installed package "apache2":

```
zypper remove apache2
```

note: no longer needed dependencies are *not* automatically removed.

example: remove the installed package "apache2" *and* the now no longer needed dependencies:

```
zypper remove --clean-deps apache2
```

example: update all installed packages to their latest available version:

```
zypper update
```

Hardware Inspection

The tools in this section can be used to collect information about the available hardware on a system.

lspci	list the available pci devices

lspci --help
man lspci
	lspci gives you a great view over the installed pci-devices on your system.
	
	Simply call lspci to get the list:
	
	```\nmax@demo:~$ lspci\n00:00.0 Host bridge: Intel Corporation 440FX - 82441FX PM(\n00:01.0 ISA bridge: Intel Corporation 82371SB PIIX3 ISA [I\n00:01.1 IDE interface: Intel Corporation 82371SB PIIX3 IDI\n00:01.2 USB controller: Intel Corporation 82371SB PIIX3 U!\n00:01.3 Bridge: Intel Corporation 82371AB/EB/MB PIIX4 ACP:\n00:02.0 VGA compatible controller: Cirrus Logic GD 5446\n00:03.0 SCSI storage controller: XenSource, Inc. Xen Plat\n```
	
	If you want to see more detailed information for each device, append one (or more) "-v".
	
	```\nlspci -v\n```

lsusb	list all available usb-devices

lsusb --help
man lsusb
	lsusb does the same as lspci but for usb-devices: show them in a list
	
	```\nmax@demo:~$ lsusb\nBus 001 Device 002: ID 0627:0001 Adomax Technology Co., L:\nBus 001 Device 001: ID 1d6b:0001 Linux Foundation 1.1 roo\n```
	
	The "-v" switch is also available but be warned about the amount of available information ;-)
	
	```\nlsusb -v\n```

lsblk	list all available block-devices
lsblk --help man lsblk	On some Linux systems lsblk is installed to give you an overview over all available block-devices.

```
max@demo:~$ lsblk
NAME      MAJ:MIN RM   SIZE RO TYPE MOUNTPOINT
sr0         11:0    1  1024M  0 rom
xvda       202:0    0    25G  0 disk
|-xvda1   202:1    0    24G  0 part /
|-xvda2   202:2    0     1K  0 part
`-xvda5   202:5    0  1022M  0 part [SWAP]
```

cat	print out system-information from files under /proc/
cat --help man cat	cat for system-information? Yes! Many system-information can be asked directly from the kernel by reading files within the /proc/ directory. **example:** get information about all available cpus / cpu-cores

```
cat /proc/cpuinfo
```

Other interesting files are for instance "/proc/meminfo", "/proc/swaps" or "/proc/interrupts".

lsmod	get a list of loaded kernel-modules
lsmod --help man lsmod	Sometimes it can be useful to know the loaded kernel-modules (aka "drivers") on a system. Use lsmod to get a list:

```
max@demo:~$ lsmod
Module                  Size  Used by
netlink_diag           16384  0
xt_nat                 16384  6
xt_mark                16384  4
xt_limit               16384  1
xt_multiport           16384  1
veth                   24576  0
...
```

modprobe	load or remove kernel-modules
modprobe --help man modprobe	Typically kernel-modules (aka "drivers") are loaded automatically if needed. If you need to do this manually, use `modprobe`. **example:** load the module "e1000" ``` modprobe e1000 ``` `modprobe` can also be used to remove an already loaded module with "-r" ``` modprobe -r lp ``` Needless to say, that the loading and unloading of kernel-modules needs root-permissions.

Network: Configuration

Every Linux-system is deeply integrated with all common network-protocols. So it is not surprising that you can find a ton of powerful tools for doing all kinds of "networking-stuff".

In this first of four networking chapters I have included the tools you need for reading or modifying the network-configuration of a system.

ip	get and modify the current ip- and routing configuration

ip --help
man ip
	ip can be used to show and configure the ip-addresses of a network-interface. Additionally this tool can be use to manage the systems route table.
	
	for managing addresses, use the "address" sub-command
	
	`ip address show`
	
	if you are as lazy as I am and you want to write less, you can shorten the word "address" to "addr" and even to "a":
	
	`ip a show`
	
	(you can even omit the "show" here, as this is the default action.
	
	example: add the IP-Address "10.0.0.1/24" to the interface "ens33":
	
	`ip a add 10.0.0.1/24 dev ens33`
	
	with the "route" sub-command, you can manage the routing-table:
	
	`ip route show`
	
	or even shorter
	
	`ip r`
	
	example: add the default gateway, which in this example is the "10.0.0.254":

```
ip route add default via 10.0.0.254
```

ifconfig	get and modify the current ip-configuration

ifconfig --help
man ifconfig
	`ifconfig` is the legacy tool found on most older systems to show and configure the IP-configuration of a network interface.
	
	notice: On modern systems this tool is completely replaced by `ip`.
	
	show the current configuration of "eth0":
	
	`ifconfig eth0`
	
	set the IP-address of "eth0" to "10.0.0.1/24":
	
	`ifconfig eth0 10.0.0.1/24`

route	get and modify the current routing-configuration
route --help man route	`route` is the legacy tool found on most older systems to show and configure the routing-configuration of a system. **notice:** On modern systems this tool is completely replaced by `ip`. **example:** show the current routing table without resolving IPs to names (note the "-n" switch):

```
max@demo:~$ route -n
Kernel IP routing table
Destination     Gateway          Genmask          Flags Met
0.0.0.0         172.31.32.1      0.0.0.0          UG    0
172.31.32.0     0.0.0.0          255.255.240.0    U     0
```

example: add a default gateway to the route table, which is here the "10.0.0.254"

```
route add default gw 10.0.0.254
```

ifup	activate a network interface
ifup --help man ifup	**ifup** is a traditional command-line tool to bring network interfaces up (aka to "activate" them). The configuration for the network-interface is read from the distribution specific configuration files, like for example "/etc/network/interfaces" on Debian based systems. Simply call this command with the name of the network interface you want to configure and activate. **example:** activate the interface "ens33": `ifup ens33`

ifdown	deactivate a network interface
ifdown --help man ifdown	**ifdown** is a traditional command-line tool to bring network interfaces down (aka to "deactivate" them). The configuration for the network-interface is read from the distribution specific configuration files, like for example "/etc/network/interfaces" on Debian based systems. Simply call this command with the name of the network interface you want to deactivate. **example:** deactivate the interface "ens33": `ifdown ens33`

cat	get the currently used DNS resolver
cat --help man cat	Ey Robert - again **cat**? YES! The currently used DNS-resolvers for your system are configured in the textfile "/etc/resolv.conf". And how can you quickly see the content of a textfile? Right - with **cat** ... ``` max@demo:~$ cat /etc/resolv.conf nameserver 8.8.8.8 nameserver 1.1.1.1 ```

Do you see the address "127.0.0.53" as nameserver on your system? This shows that your DNS-resolution is driven by a service called "systemd-resolved".

In this case you could use `cat` with "/etc/systemd/resolv.conf" or with the files located in "/run/systemd/resolve/".

notice: If your distribution runs systemd-resolved, it's often more simple to use `resolvectl`.

resolvectl	Inspect and manage the status of systemd-resolved
resolvectl --help man resolvectl	If your distribution runs "systemd-resolved", you can use `resolvectl` to show the status of this services - including detailed information about the used DNS-servers.

```
resolvectl status
```

If you want to clear the DNS-cache, use "flush-caches":

```
resolvectl flush-caches
```

Network: Analysis & Troubleshooting

This second chapter contains the tools you may need for troubleshooting and analysis.

ping	send icmp echo-request to a system (aka "ping" a host)
ping --help man ping	ping is used to send icmp echo-request packets to a system and wait for the replies (aka. to "ping" a host) ping runs until you press **<ctrl>+c** and gives you at the end statistics about the packets sent and received.

```
max@demo:~$ ping google.de
PING google.de (172.253.116.94) 56(84) bytes of data.
64 bytes from dj-in-f94.1e100.net (172.253.116.94): icmp_
64 bytes from dj-in-f94.1e100.net (172.253.116.94): icmp_
^C
--- google.de ping statistics ---
2 packets transmitted, 2 received, 0% packet loss, time 1(
rtt min/avg/max/mdev = 1.722/1.748/1.775/0.049 ms
```

if ping shall not run forever, set the number of packets to send with the "-c" switch.

```
ping -c 3 www.google.de
```

if you want to avoid resolving IP-addresses to hostnames for every incoming response-packet, add the "-n" switch.

```
max@demo:~$ ping -n www.google.de
PING google.de (172.253.116.94) 56(84) bytes of data.
64 bytes from 172.253.116.94: icmp_seq=1 ttl=58 time=1.70
64 bytes from 172.253.116.94: icmp_seq=2 ttl=58 time=1.70
^C
--- google.de ping statistics ---
2 packets transmitted, 2 received, 0% packet loss, time 1(
rtt min/avg/max/mdev = 1.704/1.704/1.705/0.041 ms
```

Hint: ping has many more useful parameters for network-troubleshooting (eg. "-t" or "-s") and can be used perfectly for automation (see the return-code via echo $?)

traceroute	determine the path a packet travels to a destination
traceroute --help man traceroute	If you want to troubleshoot routing- or performance-problems to a remote system, then `traceroute` can be used to determine the path a packet travels to the destination (alongside with the latency your

If everything works as expected, you'll see all the routers ("hops") a packet passes:

```
max@demo:~$ traceroute -n google.de
traceroute to google.de (172.217.19.67), 30 hops max, 60 |
 1  100.115.92.193  0.085 ms  0.022 ms  0.130 ms
 2  100.115.92.25  1.907 ms  0.533 ms  0.466 ms
...
14  209.85.245.203  69.025 ms  68.743 ms 69.086 ms
15  172.217.19.67  68.233 ms  67.943 ms  67.688 ms
```

The "-n" switch I used here suppresses the resolving of the IP-addresses to host-names.

Because `traceroute` by default sends udp-packets with random port-numbers, firewalls are often dropping these packets and you'll only see the hops until this dropping firewall.

If you know that packets addressed to a specified protocol/port can pass the firewall instead, you can set the protocol with "-U" or "-T" (for udp or tcp) and the port with "-p".

example: start a trace with tcp-packets to port 443

```
traceroute -T -p 443 google.de
```

host	resolve a hostname via dns and do other dns-queries
host --help man host	`host` is the most simple tool to test the DNS functionality of a system.

Call the host-command with a hostname as a parameter to resolve this name to an IP-address using the resolver of the system (see "/etc/resolv.conf"):

```
max@demo:~$ host www.google.com
www.google.com has address 216.58.213.228
www.google.com has IPv6 address 2a00:1450:4005:800::2004
```

If you want to resolve an IP-address "backwards" to a name, simply feed the host command with this address:

```
max@demo:~$ host 216.58.213.228
228.213.58.216.in-addr.arpa domain name pointer ham04s01-
228.213.58.216.in-addr.arpa domain name pointer ham04s01-
```

If you want to check the functionality of a certain DNS-server, append this server as a second parameter:

```
host www.google.com 1.1.1.1
```

The host-command can also be used to do other DNS-queries, such as for instance to retrieve the MX-records of a given domain:

```
host -t MX gmail.com
```

dig	resolve a hostname via dns and do other dns-queries
dig --help man dig	dig is a second tool to do dns-queries. The syntax of its command line is a bit different from the host command and the output gives by default more detailed information. example: query 1.1.1.1 for the MX-record for "gmail.com" `dig -t MX gmail.com @1.1.1.1`

arp	read or modify the arp-cache
arp --help man arp	To reaching systems within the local network, the mac-addresses of those systems are needed. The local arp-cache caches these addresses and can be read or modified with the arp command. example: show the local arp-cache without resolving IP-addresses

```
sudo arp -n
```

netstat	list all active or listening network ports of the local system

netstat --help
man netstat
	The command `netstat` is typically used to show active network connection of the current system or to show all the open network-ports, where processes are listening on.
	
	The most common parameters are:
	
	• -n ... do not resolve numbers to names
	• -l ... show listening ports instead of active connections
	• -t ... show tcp-ports (sockets)
	• -u ... show udp-ports (sockets)
	• -p ... show the process connected to a port (socket) (note: the processes can only be seen by root)
	
	example: show all currently active tcp-connections
	
	`netstat -ntp`
	
	example: show all listening tcp- and udp-ports
	
	`netstat -nltup`

ss	list all active or listening network ports of the local system
ss --help man ss	The command `ss` is a modern alternative to the command `netstat`. It is typically used to show active network connection of the The most common parameters are: • -n ... do not resolve numbers to names • -l ... show listening ports instead of active connections • -t ... show tcp-ports (sockets) • -u ... show udp-ports (sockets) • -p ... show the process connected to a port (socket) (note: the processes can only be seen by root) **example:** show all currently active tcp-connections

```
ss -ntp
```

example: show all listening tcp- and udp-ports together with the
processes that have opened these ports:

```
ss -nltup
```

telnet	manually open a tcp-connection to a remote host/port
telnet --help man telnet	Although "telnet" is the name for an obsolete protocol to work remotely at the command line, the client-tool `telnet` itself can perfectly be used to check if you can reach a tcp-port over the network and if the process listening there speaks the protocol you expect. Simply give two parameters to `telnet`: the host you want to reach and the port. example: Try to connect via tcp to "gmail-smtp-in.l.google.com" on port "25" and let's see if there listens an smtp-service:

```
max@demo:~$ telnet gmail-smtp-in.l.google.com 25
Trying 2a00:1450:400c:c00::1b…
Connected to gmail-smtp-in.l.google.com.
Escape character is '^]'.
220 mx.google.com ESMTP s15si637768wmc.220 - gsmtp
helo max
250 mx.google.com at your service
quit
221 2.0.0 closing connection s15si637768wmc.220 - gsmtp
Connection closed by foreign host.
```

nmap	scan a remote system for presence or open ports
nmap --help man nmap	if you want to know which ports of a remote system are reachable from the system you are currently on, you can try a "port-scan" via nmap:

```
nmap 192.168.123.123
```

nmap then tries to connect to a series of tcp-ports to determine if they are reachable or not.

If you want to scan for udp-sockets, you need to ask for a udp-scan with "-sU". But be aware that udp-scans are way slower than scans for tcp-sockets.

notice: nmap can do much more than simple ports-scans. Have a look into the documentation.

tcpdump	observe network-packets seen on an interface
tcpdump --help man tcpdump	With tcpdump you can easily see which network-packets are reaching or leaving your system:

```
tcpdump -n
```

The "-n" switch here again switches off IP-address resolving.

If your system has multiple network-interfaces, you can select the one you are interested in with the "-i" switch:

```
tcpdump -n -i ens32
```

tcpdump can always be terminated by pressing **<ctrl>+c**.

Sometimes it can be very useful to filter packets by certain criteria (host, protocol, port, ...).

```
tcpdump -n -i ens32 host www.google.com and port 443
```

If you want to analyze the captured packets with a graphical tool like wireshark, you can simply save the captured packets into a file ("-w" switch) and open this file later on with the tool of your choise.

But don't forget to capture the whole packets (typically 1500 bytes) to not miss important data for analysis:

```
tcpdump -s 1500 -w packets.log
```

Network: Transferring Data

This third network-chapter is reserved for useful tools that let you transfer data between systems.

wget	get or download data from a webserver
wget --help man wget	`wget` is a powerful tool to retrieve data from a webserver. **example:** download the content of the webpage "https://www.google.com":

```
wget https://www.google.com
```

The downloaded data (aka the website) is saved into a file in the current directory.

To explicitly specify a file where the data shall be saved, use the "-O" switch:

```
wget https://www.google.com -O google.html
```

Sometimes you may be interested in the response-headers the server sends you. You can see them with "-S":

```
wget https://www.google.com -S -O /dev/null
```

Because I'm here only interested in the response-headers, I've sent the output straight to "/dev/null", where it will instantly be forgotten.

If you don't want to see all this progress-data and debug-information, switch `wget` into "quiet-mode" with "-q".

In the following example, the content of the website is sent to `wc` which simply counts the words here:

```
wget https://www.google.com -q -O - | wc -w
```

As you can see, the special filename "-" for the switch "-O" sends the data to the output-datastream "stdout" for further processing.

notice: To learn all about the fun stuff like sending form-data, setting cookies, manipulating headers, using proxies and much more, have a look into the documentation!

curl	get or data from a webserver
curl --help man curl	`curl` is an other powerful tool for connecting with websites. As `curl` by default sends the downloaded data to the output-datastream "stdout", you have to specify a file with "-o" if you want to save the content:

```
curl -o google.html https://www.google.com
```

To see only the response-headers the server sends, use "-D -" to write them to the output-datastream stdout, throw away the data itself with "-o /dev/null" and suppress all the verbose output with the silent-mode "-s":

```
curl -o test -D - -s https://www.google.de
```

notice: to learn all about the fun stuff like sending form-data, setting cookies, manipulating header, using proxies and much more, have a look into the documentation!

nc	send a datastream over the network
nc --help man nc	`nc` stands for "net cat" and is a simple usable but powerful tool to send datastreams over the network. On the source-side you use **netcat** to generate a datatream that is send over the network. On the receiving side can be any TCP enabled service or netcat itself in "listening mode" to receive the data. **example:** open tcp-port 8080 and wait there for incoming data

```
nc -l -p 8080
```

The "-l" switch starts `nc` in listening mode.

Incoming data will be printed out to stdout. You will see them per default on your terminal.

If you want to send data to a remote network port, you have to give this data to nc on its input-datastream (stdin).

example: send "hello world" via tcp to a remote-system port 8080

```
echo "hello world" | nc 10.0.0.1 8080
```

ssh	execute remote commands or send data, connecting via ssh
ssh --help man ssh	Although ssh is typically used for opening a shell on a remote-system, it can also be used to call single commands remotely or to transfer data through the established ssh-tunnel.

example: open an shell on a remote system and try to login there as the user "max":

```
ssh max@10.0.0.10
```

example: open a ssh connection to a remote system to start there a single command:

```
ssh max@10.0.0.10 "sudo reboot"
```

example: use ssh to copy the content of a remote file to a local file:

```
ssh max@10.0.0.10 "cat /etc/passwd" > passwd_copy
```

Data can also be transferred from the local to the remote system. Simply feed the data to the input-datastream of ssh. This data can then be read remote from stdin:

```
echo "hello" | ssh max@10.0.0.10 "cat > greeting.txt"
```

scp	copy files via ssh over the network
scp --help man scp	scp is used to transfer files to or from a remote-system.

scp tries to behave like the local command cp but uses ssh to transfer data from and to remote-systems.

To address a file on a remote-system, prepend it with the address or name of the remote-system followed by a colon:

10.0.0.10:/home/max/report.txt

If you need a different username than your local one for connecting to the remote system, prepend it additionally followed by an "@"-sign:

root@10.0.0.10:/home/max/report.txt

example: copy a single file to a remote system

```
scp /etc/passwd max@10.0.0.10:/tmp
```

example: copy a complete directory from remote as backup to the local system:

```
scp -pr root@10.0.0.10:/etc /tmp/etc_backup
```

Notice in the command line above the "-p" switch to preserve meta-information and the "-r" switch to copy an entire directory recursively.

rsync	synchronize files from a source to a destination
rsync --help man rsync	If you regularly transfer the same dataset, then rsync can be very useful, as it only transfers modifications since the last transfer. rsync can connect to remote-systems using the ssh protocoll. The addressing of remote files and directories works as with scp: prepend the hostname followed by a colon to the path. **example**: The directory "/var/www" on the host "10.0.0.10": 10.0.0.10:/var/www If you need a different user for the remote-login, prepend it followed by an "@"-sign.

example: The same directory as above, but use the user "www-data" to login to the remote system:

www-data@10.0.0.10:/var/www

To really transfer every kind of files and to transfer recursively entire directories and to preserve meta-information wherever possible, use the "archive-mode" with "-a".

example: copy/sync an entire directory from a remote-system to the local directory "/srv/backup":

```
rsync -a www-data@10.0.0.1:/data /srv/backup
```

rsync does only delete files within the target, if you tell it to do so with the "--delete" switch:

```
rsync -a --delete www-data@10.0.0.10/data /srv/backup
```

User Interaction

These tools for user-interaction are typically used from within scripts.

echo	print out a message to the console

help echo
man echo
	echo is the most simple tool to print something out to the console
	
	```echo "Hello World"```
	
	to suppress the newline echo adds to every output, use the "-n" switch:
	
	```echo -n "Hello "; echo "World";```
	
	If you want to print out special characters like tabs or line breaks, you can use the "-e" command-line switch:
	
	```echo -e "Hello\tWorld\nnew line"```
	
	More placeholders for special characters can be found in the documentation via help echo

cat	generate multiline-output

cat --help
man cat
	cat can also be useful to generate multiline-output within a shell-script
	
	```cat << END```
	```Hello Shellscripter```
	```This is a multiline output :-)```
	```END```
	
	In this example a "HERE-document" is used to collect everything between "« END" and "END" and send this data altogether to the input-datastream "stdin" of cat. cat then simply prints this out all at once.
	
	The pattern "END" in this example can be any word of your choice.

printf	generate a more formatted output

help printf
 man printf
	printf lets you generate a nicely formatted output:
	
	 ```max@demo:~$ printf "pricetag: USD %05.2f\n" "9.5"```
	 ```pricetag: USD 09.50```

read	read user-input into a variable

read --help
 help read
	With read you can simply read in user-input into a variable.
	
	 By default read generates a variable called "REPLY" for storing the
	
	 example: read the user-input into a variable called "NAME":
	
	 ```read NAME```
	
	 To let the user know what you want him to input, print out a prompt with "-p":
	
	 ```read -p "What's your name again? " NAME```

dialog	read user-input with a nicer user-interface
dialog --help man dialog	If you want a better user-experience and less error-prone interfaces, consider using "dialog". With dialog you can present to the user a load of predefined input-forms. examples: • simple input-fields • password fields • calendars • file-select dialogs • yes-no-boxes • checkboxes, radiolists • ... **example:** Ask the user for its name with dialog:

```
dialog --inputbox "What's your name again?" 0 0
```

`dialog` reads in the user-input and prints it out via the error output datastream ("stderr").

So typically you will redirect the stderr of `dialog` into a file and read it later on into a variable:

```
dialog --inputbox "What's your name?" 0 0 2> name.txt
NAME=$(cat name.txt)
```

attention: I strongly advise you here to use unique, hard to predict filenames for the temporary file. Consider using `mktemp` for this.

example: ask the user to select its birthday on a presented calendar:

```
dialog --calendar "What's your birthday?" 0 0
```

note: Often you need to install the package "dialog" to use this tool.

select	generate a text-only selection-menu
help select	`select` is a shell-builtin of the bash-shell, that lets you generate simple but robust selection-menus from dynamically created data:

```
select FILE in *.sh ; do
  echo "you have selected $FILE"
done
```

the resulting output would look like this:

```
1) abc.sh
2) build.sh
3) generate.sh
4) serve.sh
#?
```

After the user has chosen an entry (by typing in the number of the entry and hitting <enter>), the commands between "do" and "done" will be triggered while the variable "FILE" will be loaded with the users choice.

wall	broadcast a message to the terminals of all logged in users
man wall	Did you ever need to reach out to all logged in users on a system? The command `wall` lets you do exactly this.

`wall` by default reads the message to send from its input-datastream "stdin":

```
max@demo:~$ echo "Hi there" | wall
```

Every user with an open terminal on the system would receive a message of the following format:

```
Broadcast message from max@demo

Hi there
```

A user can use the command `msg` to turn the reception of broadcasts from users other than "root" off:

```
max@demo:~$ mesg n
```

turn it on again and show the current state:

```
max@demo:~$ mesg y
max@demo:~$ mesg
is y
```

If you want to send a message only to members of a single group, that you can use (use on some distributions) the "-g" switch for this.

If you want to write to a single user only, try the command `write` instead.

write	send a message to the terminals of an other user
write --help man write	If you want to reach-out to another user currently logged into a system, you can use the `write` command for this.

write reads the message to send from its input-datastream stdin:

```
max@demo:~$ echo "Hi there!" | write robert
```

if the target-user has a terminal open (and hasn't disallowed incoming messages), he would receive a message of the following format:

```
Message from max@demo on pts/0 at 08:50 …

hi there!
```

a user can use the command msg to turn the reception of messages from other users than root off:

```
max@demo:~$ mesg n
```

turn it on again and show the current state

```
max@demo:~$ mesg y
max@demo:~$ mesg
is y
```

If you want to send a message to multiple users at once, have a look at the command wall instead.

Misc Tools

Here we have some very useful tools that are not included within another chapter.

date	print the current date and time, calculate with date and time

date --help
man date
	date is *the tool* if it comes to working with date and time at the commandline or within shell-scripts.
	
	date without any parameter shows the current date and time in the time zone the system is configured with.
	
	<pre>date</pre>
	If you want to see the time translated to a different timezone, set and export the variable TZ to the timezone of interest:
	
	<pre>export TZ=asia/tokyo
	date</pre>
	Often it is very useful to format the output the **date** command gives you. For this you give a "+"-sign as a parameter followed by a format-string, where placeholders can be used for single values the date command knows.
	
	example: print the date only as YEAR/MONTH/DAY
	
	<pre>max@demo:~$ date +"%Y/%m/%d"
	2024/04/10</pre>
	example: print the current date and time as unix-timestamp
	
	<pre>max@demo:~$ date +%s
	1712732496</pre>
	To calculate a date and time from a unix timestamp, use the "-d" switch with a value of "@<timestamp>":
	
	<pre>max@demo:~$ date -d @1598364380
	Tue 25 Aug 2020 02:06:20 PM UTC</pre>
	you can even calculate with **date**:

```
max@demo:~$ date -d "now + 2 hours"
Tue 25 Aug 2020 04:07:23 PM UTC
```

hwclock	read or set the hardware-clock of a system
hwclock --help man hwclock	If you use the `date` command to show or set the date and time, then you are always only dealing with the software-clock of your system. And this software-clock is initialized during system-boot with the time of the builtin hardware-clock every system has.

The tool `hwclock` lets you read and set this hardware-clock.

example: get the current date and time from the hardware-clock:

```
hwclock
```

example: set the software-clock (aka the "system-clock") from the hardware-clock:

```
hwclock --hctosys
```

example: set the software-clock from the hardware-clock, but this time force the system to read this time as "UTC":

```
hwclock --hctosys --utc
```

example: set the hardware-clock from the current time of the system-clock:

```
hwclock --systohc
```

example: set the hardware-clock from the current time of the system-clock, but this time force the system to write the time as "UTC":

```
hwclock --systohc --utc
```

note 1: Sometimes your hardware-clock shall use your local timezone instead of "UTC". Then you can force to read and write the time of the hardware-clock as "local time" by using the parameter "--localtime".

note 2: hwclock always needs root-permissions (**sudo**)

timedatectl	control time- and date-handling
timedatectl -- help man timedatectl	On systems running with "systemd", the basic aspects of the systems date & time can be controlled via `timedatectl`.

example: show current settings (including timezone):

```
timedatectl show
```

example: set the system-clock to a specific time:

```
timedatectl set-time 2024-03-10 17:18:19
```

example: get a list of available timezones:

```
timedatectl list-timezones
```

example: set the local timezone to "Atlantic/Azores":

```
timedatectl set-timezone Atlantic/Azores
```

example: enable an available NTP-service for time-synchronization:

```
timedatectl set-ntp true
```

seq	generate a sequence of numbers
seq --help man seq	Did you ever needed a sequence of numbers at the command line? The next time you can use `seq` to help you with this.

If you call `seq` with one single number as a parameter, then you'll get a sequence from "1" up to this number.

example: get a sequence from 1 to 3:

```
max@demo:~$ seq 3
1
2
3
```

With two parameters, you set the lower and upper bounds for the sequence.

example: get a sequence from 2 to 4:

```
max@demo:~$ seq 2 4
2
3
4
```

If you give tree parameters to **seq**, then the second number is the step-with for the sequence.

example: get a sequence from 4 to 2

```
max@demo:~$ seq 4 -1 2
4
3
2
```

shuf	randomize a given list

shuf --help
man shuf
	You need some randomization? Then you should have a look at shuf.
	
	In the most simple way, **shuf** reads lines from a file and prints out all the lines in a randomized order:
	
	`shuf names.txt`
	
	If you omit the filename as an argument, **shuf** reads from its input-datastream ("stdin") and randomizes those lines. In this way, you can shuffle every datastream linewise:
	
	`ls | shuf`

Sometimes it can be helpful to shuffle not the lines of a file or a datastream, but to shuffle single "words" given as command-line parameters. For this, you need the command-line-switch "-e".

example: shuffle a given list of parameters:

```
max@demo:~$ shuf -e A B C D E
B
A
C
E
D
```

If you are interested only in randomized numbers from a defined range, you don't need to give them as parameters. Instead you can use use the "-i" switch and give a lower and an upper range-limit.

The following shuffles all numbers from 5 to 10:

```
shuf -i 5-10
```

If **shuf** shall not print out all the randomized data but only a given number of values from the beginning, use "-n". With "-n 1" you'll get for instance only the first value of the randomized list.

example: pick a random number from 1 to 10:

```
max@demo: shuf -i 1-10 -n 1
6
```

sudo	run a command as a different user
sudo --help man sudo man sudoers	If you need to escalate permissions (aka to get more permissions than your current account has), try to use the **sudo** command: ``` sudo reboot ``` The configuration for **sudo** is stored within the file "/etc/sudoers". This file is only accessible as user "root" and defines which user-accounts can do which tasks in the context of which different user. In the most simple variant, a single user can run a single command (e.g. "/sbin/reboot") with root-permissions via **sudo**.

example line in /etc/sudoers: "max" can do a `sudo reboot`

```
max ALL = /sbin/reboot
```

If the user "max" shall be an administrator of the system, who can use `sudo` for everything, replace "/sbin/reboot" with the keyword "ALL":

```
max ALL = ALL
```

If you don't want to give a single user these sudo-permissions, but you want to apply the permissions to all users of a defined group "admin" for instance, replace "max" with "%admin":

```
%admin ALL = ALL
```

In intervals, `sudo` tries to authenticate the calling user by asking for its password. If you need `sudo` to escalate permissions from within a script, you can switch-off these password-requests with the "NOPASSWD:" flag.

example: give the user "www-data" the permission to reboot the system with the help of `sudo` without entering a password:

```
www-data ALL = NOPASSWD: /sbin/reboot
```

important notice: If you want to modify the sudo configuration, be really careful as you might open your system more than you intended. Read and understand the documentation and double-check your modifications.

jq	a commmand-line JSON processor
jq --help man jq	As JSON becomes more and more popular for data-exchange, there is sometimes a need for a simple to use but powerful tool to work with json data instead of plaintext datastreams. Lets say, we have the following data-file for some expermients:

```
max@demo:~$ cat data.json
{"users": [
    {"name": "Alice", "age": 28, "role": "Engineer"},
    {"name": "Bob", "age": 25, "role": "Designer"},
    {"name": "Charlie", "age": 30, "role": "Manager"},
    {"name": "Diana", "age": 22, "role": "Engineer"}
]}
```

Now let's extract only the users with the role "Engineer" by using jq with an easy to understand "select" filter.

example: print only the "name" attribute for the engineers:

```
max@demo:~$ cat data.json \
    | jq '.users[] | select(.role == "Engineer") .name'
"Alice"
"Diana"
```

(Due to space restrictions, I've split the command line here).

example: print out the name and age of each user as json-data:

```
max@demo:~$ cat data.json \
    | jq '.users[] | {name: .name, age: .age}'
{"name":"Alice","age":28}
{"name":"Bob","age":25}
{"name":"Charlie","age":30}
{"name":"Diana","age":22}
```

example: calculate the average age of all users

```
max@demo:~$ cat data.json \
    | jq '[.users[].age] | add / length'
26.25
```

watch	repeat a command line while watching its output
watch --help man watch	Sometime it can be useful to just sit back and "watch" a command working. As an example, lets say you want to observe the size of a file during an incoming data-transfer.

Typically you would repeatedly run `ls -lh` for this file to see it grow larger.

`watch` lets you exacly do this automatically. By default, `watch` calls the command line you give it as parameter every two seconds and shows you the output at the command line.

example: watch the output of `ls -lh disk.img`

```
watch ls -lh disk.img
```

the output would look like this:

```
Every 2.0s: ls -lh disk.img          Tue May  7 13:19:09 20:

-rw-rw-r-- 1 max max  1.2G May  7 13:19 disk.img
```

time	measure the time or resources a command line needs to run
man time help time	Sometimes it can be very useful to measure the time a specific command line needs to run, especially if you start optimizing a script for processing lots of data. To measure the time a command line needs to run, simply call the command with all the necessary command-line switches via the `time` command: ``` max@demo:~$ time ./my_script.sh real 0m0.712s user 0m0.507s sys 0m0.257s ``` The output of the `time` command gives you three times: • the **real time**: This is the total elapsed wall-clock time taken by the command to complete. • the **user time**: This is the total CPU time spent in user-space (outside of kernel code). • the **system time**: This is the CPU time spent within the kernel executing system calls on behalf of the command.

Did you notice that in the given example the "real time" isn't exactly the sum of "user time" and "system time"? This discrepancy is common and can be caused by effects like waiting for resources or using multiple CPU cores in parallel.

`time` can also be used to measure various other resources like memory and I/O calls.

notice: Often, there is also a shell built-in with the name `time` available. To use the real command, it is often necessary to call it via its absolute path (usually `/usr/bin/time`).

Example: Get the maximum resident memory the process used in KBytes

```
max@demo:~$ /usr/bin/time -f "%M" ./my_script.sh
2908
```

Here the "-f" parameter is used to provide a format string describing the output `time` shall generate.

For all available placeholders for the format string, have a look at the manual page.

nohup	detach a command from the terminal
nohup --help man nohup	If you want to run a long-running command in the background, then you typically will start this command with an "&" at the end of the command line - just like in this example:

```
/usr/local/bin/backup.sh &
```

Now this long running script runs in the background of your terminal and doesn't block your prompt.

But: The running script is still attached to your terminal. Thah means, if you close your session, then the script will be terminated to.

technically spoken: your running script will get a "HUP" signal that let it terminate.

By calling your command line via **nohup**, you can change this behavior:

```
max@demo:~$ nohup /usr/local/bin/backup.sh &
nohup: ignoring input and appending output to 'nohup.out'
```

Now the command runs again in the background but this time independently from your running terminal. If you close your terminal or even if you logout from the system, the script will run in the background, as long as it has access to the resources it needs.

Everything the script would print out to the terminal if run in foreground, will now be appended to a file named "nohup.out" in the current directory or in your home-directory.

If you want to place the output in a different file, use a output-redirection for this:

```
max@demo:~$ nohup /usr/local/bin/backup.sh > /tmp/backup.
nohup: ignoring input and redirecting stderr to stdout
```

Flow Control

Although the tools and patterns from this chapter can be used perfectly at the command-line, they are typically used for writing shell-scripts.

if / then / ...	implement conditional statements
help if	With the if-then-else-pattern you can run code-blocks based on the return-code of a command line:

```
if test -d /tmp/pictures
then
    ls -l /tmp/pictures
else
    echo "no pictures available"
fi
```

Here, the test-commandline is `test -d /tmp/pictures` which checks for the existence of a directory called "/tmp/pictures".

case / in / ...	do multiple pattern-checks against a single string
help case	If you have a string and want to do multiple pattern-checks against this string, use case

```
case $ANIMAL in
  spider) echo "has it six or eight legs?"
        ;;
  kitty) echo "oh how cute"
        ;;
  horse | elephant) echo "let's go for a ride :-)"
             ;;
  *) echo "don't know $ANIMAL yet"
     ;;
esac
```

for / in / ...	run a loop for a given list of elements
help for	f you want to run a loop over a given list of elements, use a for-loop:

```
for NUMBER in 1 2 3 4 5 6 7
do
    echo "the number is $NUMBER"
done
```

while	run a loop as long as an expressions is true
help while	The while-loop lets you run a command as log as a command gives you a return-code of zero ("0"):

```
while true
do
  echo "you get this line until you interrupt me :-P"
done
```

In this example **true** is used as the "test-command". And because the only purpose of **true** is to set a return-code of zero, this loop simply runs forever (or until you hit **<ctrl>+c**).

until	run a loop until a condition becomes true
help until	The until-loop in contrast runs the loop-body until a command gives zero ("0") as the return-code:

```
until false
do
  echo "until can also run forever … ;-)"
done
```

Here **false** is used as the test-command. And because the only purpose of **false** is to set a return-code not equal zero, this loop runs forever too.

Online Bonus For Book-Readers

I hope this book is as helpful to you as it is intended to be.

As a big thank you for reading this book and to optimize the value you can get out of it, I want to give you access to some carefully crafted "book bonuses".

These bonuses may vary over time, but typically they will include free additional content, heavily discounted access to content or other incentives that may be valuable for you.

To have a look at the current bonuses, go to

https://robertw.io/book-bonus

Thank you again for reading this book!

Robert

Tool Index

Made in United States
Troutdale, OR
08/19/2024

22118691R00060